1 *above* A small wooden barque of the 1870s or '80s frozen into the River Tees at Middlesborough during a very hard winter. Her jibboom has been rigged in but her sails are bent so her stay will not be long; she is nearly light and appears to be discharging the last of a cargo of timber planks through bow ports. The planks are being carried, each by two men, across the ice

2 *overleaf* Whitby in Yorkshire is one of the historic ports of Britain, particularly famous, of course, as the first home port of Captain James Cook, the greatest of all explorers. This photograph shows a wooden barquentine, almost certainly Scandinavian, discharging cargo at one of Whitby's quays

Victorian and Edwardian
SAILING SHIPS
from old photographs

BASIL GREENHILL
and
ANN GIFFARD

B.T. BATSFORD LTD
London

Also by Basil Greenhill and Ann Giffard:

Westcountrymen in Prince Edward's Isle
(American Association Award: Filmed: Televised)
The Merchant Sailing Ship: A Photographic History
Travelling by Sea in the Nineteenth Century
Women Under Sail

By Basil Greenhill:

The Merchant Schooners (2 volumes)
Sailing for A Living
Out of Appledore (with W.J. Slade)
Boats and Boatmen of Pakistan
Steam and Sail (with Rear Admiral P.W. Brock)
Westcountry Coasting Ketches (with W.J. Slade)
A Victorian Maritime Album
The Coastal Trade (with Lionel Willis)
A Quayside Camera
The Archaeology of the Boat

First published 1976

Text copyright © Basil Greenhill & Ann Giffard 1976

Printed in Great Britain by
Butler & Tanner, Frome, Somerset
for the Publishers, B.T. Batsford Ltd,
4 Fitzhardinge Street, London W1H 0AH

ISBN 0 7134 3146 6

CONTENTS

Acknowledgements
Introduction

ACKNOWLEDGEMENTS

The photographs in this book appear by courtesy of the following: Aberdeen University Library nos 4, 20, 24, 58, 60, 84; Bideford Public Library no. 53; Bristol Museum & Art Gallery nos 57, 88, 124, 126, 140; Caernarvonshire Record Office no. 7; Edinburgh Central Library no. 86; W. Eglon Shaw, the Sutcliffe Gallery no. 2; Essex Record Office no. 18; the Gillis Collection nos. 46, 47, 49, 131, 147; the Grahame Farr Collection no. 123; Graham Gullick no. 143; Ilfracombe Museum no. 132; Middlesbrough Public Library no. 1; the National Library of Wales nos 69, 71; Pembroke County Library no. 66; Ramsgate Public Library no. 26; Scarborough Public Library no. 128; Cyril Staal nos 6, 7, 16, 67; W. R. Stock no. 129; Alexander Turnbull Library, Wellington, New Zealand no. 43; D. C. Voster Collection no. 98; and the National Maritime Museum for nos 3, 5, 9, 10, 12, 17, 22, 23, 25, 27, 28, 29, 37, 38, 39, 40, 41, 42, 44, 45, 48, 50, 51, 52, 54, 55, 59, 61, 62, 63, 64, 65, 72, 73, 74, 75, 76, 77, 79, 80, 81, 82, 85, 89, 90, 91, 92, 93, 94, 96, 99, 101, 102, 103, 104, 105, 106, 107, 108, 109, 113, 114, 115, 116, 117, 118, 120, 121, 122, 125, 127, 133, 134, 135, 136, 137, 138, 139, 141, 142, 144, 145, 146, 148, 149, 150.

No. 97 is from the Library, Windsor Castle, by permission of H.M. The Queen; no. 119 was supplied by the authors and nos 8, 11, 13, 14, 15, 19, 30, 31, 32, 33, 34, 35, 36, 68, 78, 83, 87, 95, 100, 110, 111, 112, are from the publishers' collection.

To Richard and James

INTRODUCTION

Sailing ships and boats were among the most beautiful of man's purely utilitarian creations. Now working sailing ships have completely vanished, together with the whole way of life which went on around them and most of the skills associated with their building, maintenance, handling afloat and management. They were a tool of mankind for many centuries, fundamental to the development of western society. The way of life was a very old one and the skills extremely complex – to learn the handling and management of small merchant sailing ships required total immersion in the profession from a very early age. But in their extinction working sailing ships and boats have become objects of widespread popular interest. Some of this is romantic, some of it nostalgic, some of it serious interest in the technical and the social and economic history.

3 Photographs of the brigs and brigantines which carried coal cargoes regularly or from time to time from the north-east coast to London are quite rare. This one shows the brigantine *Astrea,* built in Prince Edward Island, Canada, in 1864 and owned in Sunderland, lying in Whitby harbour. She is laid up for a while and her sails have been unbent and sent down

Because the seaman has been a man apart, cut off from most of the rest of human society, the world of the sailing ship was always a mysterious one to most men and women. Now the way of life is becoming more and more remote from anything to be found in everyday experience, and the immensely complicated technicalities more and more unintelligible. Sailing ships and boats are attractive not only because some of them were beautiful but because they embody the world we have lost. It was a world in which people built great structures out of wood and iron and stone and brick, using only hand tools and man- and woman- and horse-power. A world in which people did great things as far as ships were concerned with no more than the technical skills of the carpenter, the blacksmith, the local foundry, the ropewalk and the sail loft. Then with no capital and social resources beyond those of the local community to back them, people sailed their locally-built ships all over the world. Some of them made a hard living, some did better, some made great fortunes, some starved.

The ships, mysterious and often beautiful, and the way of life, remote from modern experience but evidently with greater freedom and individual opportunity for ordinary people than we enjoy now, fascinate people today. There is a much wider popular interest in sailing ships now than there was even fifty years ago, when there were quite a few of them still around trying to make a living. There are even attempts on both sides of the Atlantic from time to time to recreate the world of the sailing ship, with passenger cruises, museum ships and some training vessels. But it cannot be done. Old ships can be restored and, providing enough thorough professional research goes into the restoration, they can provide invaluable evidence about the way of life of a vanished world, as do country houses, barns and preserved industrial environments. But the way of life which went with sailing ships can no more be revived than the life around an eighteenth-century manor, a nineteenth-century coal mine, or a medieval cathedral. The whole structure of society, of industry and commerce has changed. No modern ship can ever be a Victorian or Edwardian merchant ship manned by a crew from before the great divide of the First World War. The men spent their working lives in the ships and were absolutely dependent on them for their living. The families of the men who manned the brigs, the schooners and the ketches from the small ports illustrated in this book lived on a minute and uncertain income, often in earth- or stone-floored, two-roomed cottages, cooking their food at the best on crude iron stoves, drawing their water from a well or stream a quarter of a mile away, relieving themselves at a privy across the yard.

The Victorian and Edwardian period saw the great era of the sailing ship. When Queen Victoria ascended the throne the typical merchant vessel differed little from her ancestors of several centuries. She was built of wood, with wooden masts and spars, and rigged with natural fibres. Her hull was full and round. She could sit nearly bolt upright on the mud of a tidal harbour (and nearly all harbours were tidal), her bows were blunt and she pushed a lot of the sea in front of her as she went through it. She had a square stern into which stern windows like those of HMS *Victory* still opened. She sailed very slowly and she was very bad at sailing to windward. Her wooden spars, her natural fibre rigging, her ironwork, required the constant attention of the skilled craftsman who comprised much of her crew. As is explained in the last section of this book, each mast was in three separate parts and faced by bad weather the crew sent the upper parts and the attendant spars to the deck, thus reducing the wind resistance of the complex rigging and the turning moment of the weights far aloft. Vessels like these typical big sailing ships of history are illustrated particularly in Plate 63. These were deep sea ships, trading all over the world. Coasting and continental trades were carried on by brigs, like that in Plate 139, smacks like those on the beach at Porth Gaverne in Plate 49, and a few early schooners.

A great many factors worked to change the picture of the typical merchant vessel during Queen Victoria's reign and at sea as great a revolution took place as in the Industrial Revolution ashore. Changes in sailing ships over the period were as great as those, say, in air transport between 1930 and 1970. With the rapidly developing industrial structure ashore, the changes in the structure of world trade, and latterly the competition of steam vessels, builders and owners of large merchant sailing ships took to the new materials made available by late nineteenth-century technology. First large parts of the rigging, then hulls and finally masts and spars were made of iron, and later hulls and masts were made of steel. The result was the great square-rigged steel sailing ship of the late nineteenth and early twentieth centuries. Nowadays these late vessels are only too often regarded as typical merchant sailing ships, which they certainly were not, and dubbed with terms not in general use when the ships were thriving, 'windjammers', 'tall ships' and frequently, even the slowest and clumsiest, as 'clippers'.

These last vessels survived through the immense strength of their steel hulls, masts, yards and wire rigging. The upper masts were not sent down in bad weather, the sails were furled along the tops of the yards and if this could not be done in time they blew into fragments, usually long before the immensely strong rigging was in danger. They still required greatly skilled crews. These were men with a technical competence which now has been completely lost, men who were required to work in industrial conditions totally unacceptable in the modern world.

Entirely new rigs developed, new dispositions of masts, spars and canvas, some of them much more efficient than any that had existed in the world before, particularly in the United States where the great multi-masted schooners, extremely efficient carriers in the trades for which they were designed, were developed. In Britain and Europe a similar revolution took place, partly under North American influence, among small merchant sailing vessels. Small ships, because they continued to be built locally of wood, by no means altogether lost their link with the typical sailing ships of the past, but their rigging was revolutionised and changed from the square-rig of the brig Plate 139) and the huge fore-and-aft sails of the smack (Plate 147) to the schooner and the ketch, (Plates 141 and 146) which became almost universal. Many of the photographs in this book do not illustrate these big and relatively big merchant sailing ships, but rather the fishing vessels and boats, and the local craft, the barges which were as much a part of the rural scene as the farm carts and road wagons to which they were complementary.

The sailing ship succumbed, slowly but steadily, in the last quarter of the nineteenth century and in Edwardian times, not only to the steam ship but to the general expansion of industrial activity, the greater degree of organisation of the world and the changing patterns of business. Almost no commercial sailing vessels, except for large North American schooners, were built after the death of Edward VII. But they were a very long time in dying out of use. The large square-rigged sailing ship ceased to be a serious factor in ocean transport after the First World War, though the big schooners lasted somewhat longer in the North American coasting trade. The last British sailing fishing fleets died out finally in the 1930s. London River sailing barges, schooners and ketches, lingered on, often with the aid of auxiliary engines, in relatively large numbers in the home trade around Britain until the Second World War. Almost incredibly, a few of them went on working until the early 1960s. So it is true that in Britain the merchant sailing vessel lasted into the space age.

Readers of this book may wonder where examples of vessels and boats of the kind illustrated here, can still be seen. There are a surprising number of sailing vessels and boats preserved around the world. Just as in Britain in the National Maritime Museum we have the world's largest and most comprehensive museum of its kind, so in Britain more old merchant ships have been preserved than anywhere else, mainly by the Maritime Trust, which has, among other vessels, the full-rigged ship *Cutty Sark* in dry dock at Greenwich, the three-masted schooner *Kathleen & May* in Sutton Harbour, Plymouth, the London River sailing barge *Cambria* at Rochester, the sailing trawler *Provident* sailing out of Salcombe in Devon, and the pilot cutter *Kindly Light* at Cardiff. The National Trust and the National Maritime Museum are at the time of writing far advanced with the restoration of the ketch *Shamrock* at Cotehele Quay near Plymouth. The Ulster Folk Museum has the three-masted schooner *Result* under restoration, while the three-masted wooden steam auxiliary barque *Discovery* is now a naval training vessel moored on the Thames Embankment in London.

Abroad, the world's oldest merchant ship, the whaling barque *Charles W. Morgan*, is preserved afloat and in excellent condition at Mystic, Connecticut. Built in 1841 at Fairhaven near New Bedford, Massachussetts, she is the only vessel left in the world which conveys what the merchant sailing ships of early Victorian times, and for a century or more before, were really like. The British-built four-masted steel barque *Pommern* is to be seen at Mariehamn in Finland and the steel barque *Star of India* at San Diego in California. The Danish three-masted schooner *Fulton*, owned by the Danish National Museum and in magnificent condition, sails among the Danish islands each summer. These are the gems of the world's collections, the vessels which have been little changed, if at all, from their merchant ship configuration. There are a number of others changed in greater or lesser degree or restored more or less well.

It is quite impossible to write a book about sailing ships without using technical terms. We have kept these to a minimum in this text but, of course, we have already had to use them fairly liberally. For those who want to know the ones that really matter, the definitions of the various rigs as they were understood in late Victorian and Edwardian times and the basic facts about masts and sails, these are explained in simple terms and illustrated in the last section of this book, with some especially attractive photographs of vessels under sail and at anchor.

Not every photograph in this book was taken in Victorian and Edwardian times, though the great bulk of them were. The surviving ships did not change in the early years after the end of the era and there are a few photographs taken a little later which still show the ships as they were at that brief and untypical time in our history when we were the world's greatest maritime and industrial power.

THE EAST COAST

This was the area particularly associated with the coal trade from the north-east to London, which employed small merchant sailing ships in their hundreds. Life in the coal trade is graphically described from firsthand experience in two books by the first Lord Runciman, *Collier Brigs and their Sailors* and *Before the Mast and After*. Despite the numbers in which they existed, photographs of the north-east coast sailing colliers are surprisingly rare but one typical vessel sailing from Whitby is shown in a photograph from the Frith Collection at the National Maritime Museum. The east coast was also the home of the great sailing fishing fleets of Yarmouth, Lowestoft, Grimsby and Hull, and the local fishing industry of many small harbours, beaches and cracks in the rocks in between these places. The fishing industry under sail has been depicted in a number of books, both contemporary and retrospective.

4 A great fleet of herring drifters gathered at Scarborough in the 1890s. Notice the horse going into the water with its rider to retrieve one of the bathing machines

5 *opposite top* The distinctive shape of the Yorkshire and Northumberland coble fishing boat can clearly be seen in this photograph of the *Rapid* and a group of her sisters of different sizes at Scarborough with a great fleet of mixed sailing drifters, trawlers and steam fishing vessels gathered in the harbour behind. It was taken on 12 April 1898

6 *opposite bottom* The coble from the north-east coast of England was one of the most distinctive of British working boats. Designed for launching into surf, she was equipped with a tall narrow dipping lug and oars set on a single thole pin. This coble with a freight of passengers is sailing off the beach at Filey in Yorkshire while another one sails parallel to the beach offshore

7 *above* This study was taken at Filey in August 1892. The most likely explanation of the scene is that a member of the crew of the ketch-rigged sailing trawler at anchor in the bay is about to be taken off to her with a can of fresh milk

8 Cobles normally employed in the local inshore fishery taking passengers out for a sail from Bridlington on a brilliant summer's day just before the First World War

9 By the entrance to Prince's Dock, Hull, a different kind of sailing ship from any other illustrated in this book is lying. She is a Humber keel with one mast setting a single squaresail on it. These keels were the traditional sailing barges of the Humber

10   *right* This photograph of Grimsby shows
steamers and big square-rigged sailing vessels all
mixed up in the dock, a sight which was
normal in late Victorian times when the picture
was taken. The sailing vessel in the left
foreground is Scandinavian, probably
Norwegian, one of the small wooden barques
which were an important part of the world's
merchant shipping in the second half of the
nineteenth century

11   *right* The docks at Boston in Lincolnshire. There are at least six sailing vessels loading and
discharging cargo and the mast of a steamer rigged with a staysail and gaff sail, which seems to be causing
a good deal of interest, in the immediate foreground. The vessel on the right-hand side is somewhat
unusual in the arrangement of her decks; she is a big two-masted schooner, probably from the
northern part of the Baltic

12   *top*   The Norfolk wherry was a shallow, usually clinker-built boat about 50 feet long and perhaps 12 feet wide, with short decks fore and aft separated by a great hatchway with very high coamings. She had a single mast from which was set a big loose-fitted square-headed gaff sail. This photograph shows wherries on Braydon Water in March 1897. The one nearest the camera is carrying a huge deck cargo

13   *above*   The Norfolk wherry *Meteor* of Surlingham discharging coal into carts one winter's day. Note that the wherryman's wife is on board; she is almost in the centre of the picture, behind the man with the sack on his back. A child stands on the foredeck

14 This is the first of three studies of Lowestoft sailing fishing vessels. Here is the harbour at Lowestoft. It was taken at a time, the 1870s or early 1880s, when Lowestoft vessels, because of the introduction of trawling, were being converted from the traditional dipping lug rig to ketch rig, or a combination of lug and ketch. The vessel in the foreground was evidently built as a lugger, but has been given a gaff mainsail. Gradually these luggers were replaced with ketches as new vessels were built

15 A group of sightseers on the end of the pier is watching the big powerful ketches which replaced the old luggers at Lowestoft leaving the harbour, four of them with the assistance of one tug which will drop them as soon as they are well clear of the pier heads

16 *right* This photograph was taken on 15 August 1890, from the pier head at Lowestoft. It shows a paddle tug towing out a big ketch-rigged trawler; the end of her beam trawl is clearly visible on the port side of the transom counter

17 *below* On the beach at Southwold in the 1880s are small inshore fishing boats, the one in the immediate foreground rigged with a dipping lug main and standing lug mizzen. This was an attractive and efficient rig for a small boat, much favoured by inshore fishermen in the Victorian era, though quite unlike the sails anybody would put on such a boat today

18 The London River sailing barge with her distinctive hull shape and equally distinctively-shaped brown tan sails is fortunately still with us in some numbers as a pleasure vessel, but it was as cargo carriers that thousands of them earned their living in Victorian and Edwardian times. Here is a group of them loading and discharging at Hythe Quay, Colchester, at about the turn of the century

19 The London River sailing barge *Mayflower* is loading corn in bags from farmers' carts at the quay at Bradwell-on-Sea in Essex in the early years of this century

THE SOUTH-EAST

The south-east, of course, includes London, greatest of British ports during the period covered by this book. Here sailing ships of every kind and description came to load and discharge cargo. The arrival of one of them after a voyage from Bombay is described in the concluding pages of Joseph Conrad's *The Nigger of the Narcissus*. The local vessel of the south-east was the London River spritsail barge, a type of efficient, economical, shallow draught, cargo carrier which was built in great numbers and in the later years of the nineteenth century was used to move cargoes far up the east coast and along the south coast as well as in the Thames and its estuary. (*See overleaf for caption to this illustration.*)

20 *previous spread* From the appearance of the
paddle steamer with the tall thin funnel in the
background this photograph of London River
sailing barges lying at anchor off Honduras
Wharf and St Paul's is a good deal older than it
looks at first glance. Such a sight as this, of
course, was common right up into the 1930s but
will never be seen again. The nearest barge is the
Pall Mall, the other is the *Our Boys*

21 *above* One misty day, probably in the 1860s,
an unknown photographer took this photograph
of Cannon Row, Westminster, with a clinker-
built coasting smack lying on the river bank
discharging sacks into a cart. Two empty wagons
stand on the cobbles

22 A London River barge, the *Alfred*, is discharging her cargo into carts driven down on to the river bank where she is beached at low tide. This is one of our favourite pictures in this book, emphasising, as it does, the direct connection between the sailing barge and the community she served. The *Alfred*, dating from the 1840s, is a 'stumpy' barge, that is without the tall topmast many of these vessels carried

23 *above* The London River barge was a highly adaptable and efficient vehicle in her day, able to carry a big cargo of coal, like the *Dawn* being discharged here, right up river to Kingston and to operate around the coasts of Kent and Essex and Suffolk as well

24 *opposite* A big London River sailing barge has a cargo of barrels, while the barge *Thirza Little*, astern of her, is now light. The big handsome brigantine which is also without cargo and drying some of her sails is probably Scandinavian. The setting is the Medway at Rochester

25 *above* During a very heavy winter in the 1890s this smack and two schooners and a ketch were frozen in for a while. Notice how the ice has collected around the flukes of the anchor and the little smack in the foreground

26 *below* Ramsgate on a wet day teems with activity. A big square-rigged sailing ship is lying at the quay right alongside the road. She may have come from anywhere in the world, but certainly from overseas since vessels of this type were not employed in the coasting trade

27 The 'yacht' *Sunbeam* of Margate collecting a freight of passengers at the pier one sunny day at the end of the Edwardian period. Most places with pretensions to being resorts had these big sailing vessels which took passengers around the bay, in this case for one shilling, 'refreshments served on board'

THE SOUTH COAST

The south coast is associated particularly with the packet trade to France from the Channel ports, which very early passed into the hands of steam ships. Great sailing ships were built at Southampton, but the port was particularly concerned with the trans-Atlantic passenger liners in their hey-day. But fishing and trading in sailing vessels continued throughout the period covered by this book, and some of this was world wide. The little barque *Britannia*, for instance, built at Shoreham in Sussex in 1877, sailed in her short life of six years to the West Indies, to India, Burma and Ceylon, to the Falkland Islands and the west coast of South America, to Boston and to New York, then to South Africa and Australia, back to Mauritius and then to Liverpool. From Liverpool she sailed to Jamaica and on her next voyage towards Canada she was lost on Sable Island.

28 The brig *Pelican* lying on the beach at Hastings. She appears to be deep laden; when the tide ebbs she will discharge into carts the coal cargo she has brought down from the north-east coast. She belonged to local coal merchants and was one of a fleet of brigs which served this part of the south coast. She stayed in the trade for at least 30 years before she was wrecked on the beach in 1879

29 *top* From about 1870 until the general adoption of motors just before the First World War, the Hastings fishing fleet comprised burdensome two-masted clinker-built boats with big dipping lugs on the foremast. They were unusual among British working boats in that they were fitted with drop keels. This is the Hastings lugger *Happy Return* lying bows on to the shingle. Notice the lamps for night fishing each lugger carries on her mizzen mast

30 *above* There was an extensive local fishing industry from Brighton, conducted in vessels not unlike the Hastings luggers seen in Plate 29. This photograph taken on the beach at Brighton in 1871 shows fishermen together with a more prosperous individual wearing a top hat, who is probably a fish merchant and proprietor. Notice the short clay pipes

31 Part of the fishing fleet lying on the beach at Brighton with nets spread out to dry on the shingle. The capstans in the foreground were used for pulling the boats up the beach. All these vessels are rigged with the old dipping lug sails, which were most commonly used by inshore fishermen throughout the period covered by this book

32 *above* The old paddle tug *Mistletoe,* a clinker-built wooden vessel, lies alongside the Russian three-masted barquentine *Siiwo Abo* at Southwick in Shoreham Harbour in 1890

33 *left* This River Ouse barge is bound for Lewes from Newhaven in Sussex. She is sprit-rigged and is typical of the extremely simple types of sailing vessel used on a number of rivers in Britain before motor transport replaced them

34 Littlehampton harbour taken in the 1890s with two brigantines and a topsail schooner lying at the quay. The latter is drying her sails

35 *above* The Edwardian era was in some ways the high period of yachting. This photograph, taken shortly before the First World War, shows the end of Ryde pier with a ketch-rigged yacht built on sailing trawler lines with great gaff sails, a long running bowsprit and ratlines on the shrouds for the men to go aloft to set the huge gaff topsail

36 *opposite* Poole quay in Dorset, now a yachting centre, lined with merchant sailing vessels loading and discharging cargo. The fine German steel schooner *Alma Elisabeth* of Hamburg is right in the foreground. The French ketch *Mesance* of Granville lies immediately ahead of her with the British ketch *Beatrice Hannah* of Gloucester, built at Bridgwater in 1888, alongside. In the background on the other side of the river is a big wooden three-masted barque

THE SOUTH-WEST

The south-west of England has, of course, been associated with maritime enterprise, with fishing, with coastal traffic and with overseas trade for centuries. It is not widely realised that although the relative importance of the area greatly diminished during the Victorian period, considerable overseas trade, particularly with North America, was maintained throughout the nineteenth century. Indeed until the First World War the building of small wooden sailing ships continued. Because of the attractions of the area for holiday makers who carried cameras the south-west is exceptionally well covered in the great collection of historic maritime photographs at the National Maritime Museum.

37 *this spread* The most famous fishing port in south-western Britain was of course Brixham, where it is sometimes claimed that trawling was invented. By the early years of Queen Victoria's reign Brixham was one of the most prosperous places on the shores of the English Channel and her fishing enterprise led to the establishment of the industry at many of the big North Sea ports. By the end of the century the Brixham trawler had developed into the largest and most powerful of British sailing fishing craft. This photograph was taken immediately before this era in the early 1880s and shows a smack-rigged Brixham trawler outward bound

38 *top* The tidal rivers, harbours, creeks and little coves of south Devon and south Cornwall were served by coasting smacks and sailing barges like this one, the *Sweet May*, built by Fred Hawke at Plymouth in the 1890s

39 *above* We have put in this slightly damaged old photograph of the ketch *Shamrock* of Plymouth because the vessel, built at Plymouth by Fred Hawke in 1899, was found, derelict and rotting but just able to be saved, in a Devon creek in 1973. She was presented to the National Trust and is now being rebuilt and restored as she was as a working sailing vessel by the National Trust and the National Maritime Museum at the Trust's Cotehele Quay on the River Tamar. When she is finished she is to sail again, so it will be possible to see one of the vessels in this book as she was in the last years of Queen Victoria's reign

40 This is one of our favourite sailing ship photographs. It shows the west country sailing barge *Myrtle*, built in the 1890s, lying in the old dock at Cotehele Quay on the River Tamar, while a man aloft in a bo'sun's chair scrapes down the mast and her owner-master, Captain Bill Martin, in peaked cap, stands on the foredeck. The *Myrtle* brought the groceries for the great house at Cotehele and the neighbouring villages and hamlets once a week. She brought corn for Cotehele watermill, as well as coal and fertiliser. She was as much a part of the local rural scene as the farm wagons and the lime kilns on the quay. The National Trust owns the Cotehele Estate and they have restored the house, the quay, the dock, the watermill and the sailing barge *Shamrock*, (see Plate 39) to show the life of a local community on a great tidal river during previous centuries

41 *above* Calstock in Cornwall was a thriving shipping place for most of the nineteenth century. This photograph, taken in the 1890s or earlier, shows three big schooners and a coasting smack lying off the old quays, the ruins of which can still be seen rising from the mud of the river today

42 *below* Fowey in Cornwall is today a place of export of vast quantities of china clay. Eighty years ago clay was already being exported coastwise and overseas, mainly in sailing ships. Here in the immediate foreground the ketch *Surprise* is being loaded by a little mobile steam crane with a cargo probably bound for the north-west coast. Out in the river a great wooden full-rigged ship waits to load her cargo, probably for the United States

43 *above* Throughout the Victorian era and well into the present century small wooden sailing ships were still carrying cargoes of one or two hundred tons all over the world. This is the barquentine *Ocean Ranger* in dry dock in Port Chalmers, New Zealand. She was built at Appledore in North Devon in 1875 and owned in Fowey in Cornwall

44 *below* Pentewan, along the coast from Fowey, was also a place of export of china clay to coastal and continental ports. It is nowadays completely silted up, but when this photograph was taken at the beginning of this century it was a thriving shipping place. This photograph shows five big schooners and a ketch

45 The harbour at Porthleven filled with small fishing vessels. The little trading ketch *Ann Elizabeth* of Penzance, built at Hastings in 1856 and owned in Plymouth, lies at the quayside

46 This fleet of luggers lies in Mounts Bay off Newlyn. The catch is coming ashore in boats and being loaded into two-wheeled carts on the tide line and in the water. This is a very old photograph, taken before the building of the new quay walls at Newlyn in 1885–8. Much of the area occupied by the fishing fleet was enclosed by the nineteenth-century harbour

47 *above* An interested group of spectators on the end of the breakwater watch a fleet of luggers putting to sea one calm misty morning from Newquay, Cornwall. The vessels have worked out under their great sweeps and are setting sail as they leave the harbour mouth. One of them, the *Snowdrop*, of Penzance, in the right foreground, is still being pulled. They are a mixed bunch of boats, some at least from Porthleven on the south coast (see Plate 45)

48 *opposite top* The preceding photograph showed a fleet of fishing luggers sailing out of Newquay harbour. This one shows a big two-masted schooner, the *Fairy Maid*, built in the Gannel, near Newquay, in 1876, sailing right into the harbour. The area available inside is very small and the vessel is sailing fast through the narrow gap between the piers. Seamanship of this order was a normal attainment in the late nineteenth century. With the departure of the necessity for them skills of this kind have now completely vanished

49 *opposite bottom* Coasting smacks lying on the beach at Porth Gaverne in North Cornwall. The middle one is the *Telegraph*, built at Porth Gaverne in 1859. The smack nearest the camera is discharging coal down a shute into carts. This is the way in which many communities received their coal and other supplies in the days before motor lorries

THE BRISTOL CHANNEL

It was in the Bristol Channel ports and trades that the small wooden sailing ship survived the longest. Great fleets of schooners and ketches were still sailing from North Devon and to some extent from the Somerset coast right through the Edwardian era. Schooners continued to be built at Appledore until three years after the death of King Edward VII. The Bristol Channel was the home of the coasting ketch, the last type of small wooden merchant sailing ship to be developed. These efficient and economical vessels found work to do around the ports of the south-west until the Second World War.

50 *opposite* This is Appledore quay at the beginning of this century. Isaac Croner, sailing barge hand, stands with his back to the camera on the right. William Short, also a sailing barge hand, is on the left. The boy visitor is taking his little sister down the slipway. The trading smack alongside the quay is the *Rosamond Jane*, built at Padstow in 1834, the last vessel to trade into Hartland quay before it was destroyed by gales in the 1890s

51 *above* Measuring an anchor chain on Appledore quay. Two of the local sailing bargemen look on and a boy, who, because he is wearing boots and socks, is probably a visitor rather than a local boy – most of the local boys went barefooted on week days – looks on. The vessels are from left to right, the ketch *Emu*, the ketch *Advance*, and the ketch *Wolf* built at Fowey in 1862, all locally owned in Appledore. The *Wolf* was built to carry granite blocks for the construction of the Wolf rock lighthouse. As soon as the contract was completed she was bought by an Appledore owner.

52 *above* The Appledore sailing barge *Nellie*, built at Cleave Houses near Bideford, in a flat calm off the Appledore shipyard. The boy in the boat is taking her line over to a mooring buoy which was kept for the use of the barges off the shipyard. The photograph was taken at the beginning of this present century

53 *opposite top* Bideford quay in the 1860s before the widening of the later nineteenth century, with a group of local vessels. There is a schooner, three coasting smacks, two or three local rowing barges, and a local sailing barge called the *Lady of the Lake*, which was possibly a vessel of that name built at New Bideford in Prince Edward Island, Canada, in the early 1820s. In the foreground is a polacca brigantine, the *Jane & Mary*, built at Bideford in 1827.

54 *opposite bottom* The same quay about 50 years later. The first car to be owned in the port of Bideford is travelling south, in the middle of the road, in the early years of this century. Two ketches lie alongside the quay, the one nearest the camera with her discharging gear rigged is the *Clara May*, built at Plymouth in 1891 and owned in Bude, Cornwall, at the time this photograph was taken. Apart from the amount of traffic, Bideford quay has changed relatively little since then and Scandinavian motor vessels still discharge cargoes of timber in the berth in which the *Clara May* is lying

55 The schooner *Colleen*, built at Barnstaple in 1880, the ketch *Humility*, built at Littlehampton in 1839, and the ketch *Acacia*, built at Plymouth in 1880, being towed to sea from Appledore Pool in North Devon behind the steam tug *Times*

56 This photograph of Lynmouth in North Devon shows a ketch lying aground on a shingle bank discharging her cargo of sacks into a cart. A smack, the *Mary* of Bideford, built at Chepstow in 1817, is waiting to discharge a cargo which includes a large number of barrels carried on deck. Lynmouth, like dozens of other small harbours and beaches around the coast of Britain, was regularly served by small sailing vessels like these which brought the essentials for the local community and took away the products of the local agriculture and industry

57 *above* This photograph shows the schooner *Flower of the Fal* towing through Cumberland Basin in Bristol, watched by interested groups who appear to be out for a Sunday afternoon's walk. The *Flower of the Fal* was built at Padstow in 1870 and owned in Falmouth. She was employed for some time in the Newfoundland trade, frequently being chartered to take cargoes of salted cod to Bristol. In 1891 she was forced to give up a voyage from Bristol to Harbour Grace and run back to Falmouth, having lost both her charter and most of her canvas after 60 days of struggle

58 *opposite* A wooden three-masted barque, almost certainly from the details of her construction built in Canada, lying alongside St Augustine's Parade in Bristol. The photograph was taken late in Victorian times and among other items of interest contains a horse tram. This part of Bristol docks is now completely covered over and although some of the buildings here are still recognisable, the area where the ships were lying is given over to an endless stream of cars and buses

59 *right* A coasting smack and a coasting ketch, each behind a tug, towing from King Road off Portishead on the Somerset coast up the estuary of the Severn, bound to Sharpness or to Gloucester. They are probably not local vessels, regular traders, or they would have sailed up and saved the expense of the tug. They are not bound for Lydney, for if they were their tow ropes would be over the port bow to enable them to be slipped easily by the tug in the strong flowing tide off the entrance to the dock, after which they warped into the basin. The navigation of the Severn estuary by sailing vessels was an extremely skilled business requiring considerable local knowledge

60 *below* The docks at Gloucester filled with sailing ships all drying their sails. A Norwegian barque, the *Arco* of Drammen, and a French schooner, the *Dauphinelle* of Vannes, lie in the foreground. Immediately beyond them are two Severn trows, the local sailing barges peculiar to the Bristol Channel

61 *above* A Bristol Channel pilot cutter
photographed in the 1890s. The cruising ground
of some of the Bristol Channel pilots was between
Scilly and the south of Ireland. Their seeking
grounds were open to North Atlantic gales and
greatly affected by tides. Their life was a hit and
miss existence dependent on good fortune in
meeting inward bound shipping, but the Bristol
Channel ports were prosperous and vessels
frequent and on the whole pilots were among the
more highly paid of professional seamen

62 Barry docks in the 1890s, filled with great steel sailing ships and their direct competitors, bulk-carrying steamers of approximately the same size. Almost all these vessels have come to load coal to be carried to ports all over the world

WALES

The Welsh ports can be sharply divided. The coal ports of the south attracted sailing ships to load cargoes which they took all over the world. This was a trade which played a large part in British economic prosperity and expansion in the Victorian era. The ports of west and north Wales were the home of fleets of small sailing vessels, nearly all built of wood, which also traded very widely overseas as well as on the coast. The remarkable history of Porthmadog and the ports of Anglesey has recently been recorded by Mr Aled Eames. Porthmadog's period of prosperity, indeed of very existence as a shipping place, roughly spans the Victorian and Edwardian period. In these years her great fleet of sailing ships traded all over the world, latterly most particularly in the Newfoundland trade with salt fish for the Mediterranean, the Iberian Peninsula and Britain. For this trade a type of three-masted schooner was developed. These vessels were perhaps the finest small merchant sailing ships ever built in this country.

63 *opposite top* Swansea in the days when the harbour still dried out on almost every tide. This photograph taken in the early 1840s shows a very different world from that of the great steel sailing ships of the late nineteenth century. This vessel is far more typical of the sailing ship in her long unchallenged years as a tool of expanding commerce in the eighteenth and early nineteenth centuries. Notice that she and the vessel lying forward of her have both been rigged down, that is, their upper masts and yards have been sent down on deck. This does not mean that they were laid up or being dismantled. With wooden masts and spars and natural fibre rigging this kind of extensive overhaul was regularly given by their own crews to vessels in dock

64 *opposite bottom* These are Swansea Bay pilot schooners, used by the pilots who served the vessels shown in the last photograph, in about 1845. They are a remarkable survival, with the masts and sails of the seventeenth-century shallop or two-mast boat, the ancestor of the schooner, which became so popular in the nineteenth century

65 *above* This photograph of Prince of Wales dock, Swansea, on 31 May 1894, is separated from the last two by a technical revolution reflected in almost every visible detail. The sailing ships have altered out of all recognition to the great steel vessels of the last quarter of the nineteenth century, which were in no way typical of the merchant sailing ship for the greater part of her history. The two big sailing vessels in the foreground are the iron four-masted full-rigged ship *Falls of Foyers*, built in 1883 at Greenock, and the steel barque *Inverlyon*, built in the early 1890s at Port Glasgow and lost through collision with the German barque *Khorasan* in mid-Atlantic

66 Vessels from Brixham in Devon fished all around the coasts of England and in the summer based themselves on harbours far from their home port. This photograph (probably taken in the 1880s) shows a fleet of Brixham trawlers in Tenby. They are drying their nets on a summer's day. Other trawlers, both smack- and ketch-rigged, lie out in the bay

67 These Brixham trawlers are lying in shallow
water at the side of the entrance to Tenby
harbour. Some members of the crew of one of
them have come ashore by boat and they are now
pushing the boat off to rejoin their vessel. It is
2 August 1897

68 It seems almost unbelievable today, but in the mid-nineteenth century the little harbour of Nefyn in Gwynedd was a shipbuilding centre. The first vessel known to have been built there was launched in 1760; the last, the schooner *Venus*, in 1880. Square-rigged sailing ships were built here. Three schooners are here seen under construction and a smack is undergoing repair on the beach in the middle of the picture

69 One of the great shipping places of Wales was Porthmadog in Gwynedd. A creation of the early nineteenth century, its ships sailed all over the world, especially with slate from the local quarries to European ports and with salted cod fish from Newfoundland to the Mediterranean, Portugal, Spain and Britain. Only one vessel in this photograph can be identified: under the jib boom of the schooner in the foreground is the little schooner *Physician* of Pwllheli, built at Pwllheli in 1862

70 *opposite top* The slate trade was the heart of Porthmadog's prosperity. Here slates are being loaded into a schooner lying at Greaves Wharf. They are probably for export to Germany

71 *opposite bottom* Port Dinorwic in Gwynedd was also a great centre for the export of slate, here shown awaiting shipment

72 *above* Connah's Quay on the Dee in Flintshire was once a centre of sailing ship trade and the home of a great fleet of sailing vessels. The last wooden merchant schooner to remain afloat, the *Kathleen & May*, preserved at Plymouth by the Maritime Trust, was built here in the last year of the last century. This photograph was taken earlier and illustrates the origin of the expression 'a forest of masts and spars'

THE NORTH-WEST

Liverpool was, of course, the great sailing ship port of western England in the Victorian/Edwardian period, but there was a great deal of shipping activity of various kinds all the way from the Mersey to the Scottish border. Maryport and Workington were deeply involved in international trade. Schooners traded across the Solway Firth and the largest of all the fleets of schooners were owned in Barrow and in Millom. Great fishing fleets sailed from Fleetwood and the Isle of Man which had its own shipbuilding industry. Indeed, the iron barque *Star of India*, built in the island, which once carried emigrants to New Zealand, is still preserved fully rigged at San Diego in California.

73 The docks on the Mersey were filled with great sailing ships in the latter part of the Victorian era. This is Langton dock on 20 April 1895. The vessel in the centre of the picture is the three-masted wooden barque *Edward Wake*, while to the right of her lies a Scots vessel, the three-masted wooden barque *Good Intent* of Montrose, built at Montrose in 1869

74 Liverpool docks in the 1890s: Salthouse dock with three large steel barques and the attendant flotilla of barges and lighters, taken on 9 April 1895

75 Runcorn was a great port for schooners in the period covered by this book. They brought china clay from Cornwall for the Potteries and left with coal for all the harbours of western Britain. There is a very good description of the sailing of the Runcorn fleet in John Masefield's book *New Chum*. This photograph shows the docks with a number of schooners

76 *left* The Isle of Man was once the home of great sailing fishing fleets: Port Erin in the early 1890s with local luggers

77 *below* Maryport, crammed so full with small wooden merchant sailing vessels that it is not possible to count them. From the rigging of the vessels it is unlikely that this photograph was taken after the 1860s and it may well date from the '50s

78 Maryport was the birthplace of a number of fine sailing ships in the Victorian era. The *Southerfield*, built at Maryport in 1881, ready for launching

79 Communication on the west coast of Scotland used to be largely by sea and there were many places entirely dependent on the water for their link with the outside world. Before the development of the small steam ships, the Clyde puffers, this trade was carried on by coasting smacks and ketches and some of these vessels went on trading until the 1930s. This photograph shows the *Maggie*

SCOTLAND

People knowledgeable in the history of sailing ships associate Scotland at once with the great shipbuilding industry of the Clyde and the great steel full-rigged ships and four-masted barques of the later years of Queen Victoria's reign. A number of these vessels are illustrated in this book in photographs taken in other parts of Britain. Besides these great ships there were dozens of schooners sailing from Scottish ports, coasting smacks which served the little harbours of the Western Isles, great fleets of sailing fishing vessels, and fully-rigged steam whalers, some of which went to the ultimate ends of the earth as exploration ships.

80 *above* The vessel on the left in this photograph is one of a type built to trade through the Forth and Clyde canal, locally known as a gabbart; the vessel on the right is another of the west coast trading smacks with her topmast housed

81 *below* In the late years of Queen Victoria's reign more efficient and more economical rigs began to be adopted for large sailing vessels. The Americans were very successful with big multi-masted schooners and barquentines and some British owners followed their example, though the building of new big sailing ships ceased soon after. This handsome vessel is the four-masted barquentine *Westfield*, one of five similar vessels built at Port Glasgow in the 1890s and owned in Dundee

82 *above* Lerwick about 1899, showing the mixed vessels of a great fishing fleet. They are luggers, ketches and smacks and they make a sight, once commonplace on the fishing grounds and off the fishing harbours, which is now almost beyond living memory.

83 *below* Pulteneytown Harbour, Wick, with a great fishing fleet in harbour and a small fleet of schooners lying at the dockside to take away the products of the fishery, herrings packed in barrels

84 Aberdeen in 1882. Only one or two steamers are seen and there are at least 16 square-rigged sailing vessels

85 *opposite top* Aberdeen harbour in the late nineteenth century, filled with sailing ships of every kind, in the foreground the whaler *Hope*, built in 1873. Notice that she is a fully-rigged sailing vessel with a funnel. These steam-and-sail vessels were very successful whalers and sealers, and a number of them were used as exploration ships, of which the most famous was Captain Scott's *Terra Nova*

86 *opposite bottom* This photograph was taken by the great D.O. Hill and shows St Andrews fishwives in the middle of the nineteenth century

87 *above* These Scots fishermen were photographed in the 1840s. Notice that they wear a kind of uniform: canvas trousers, short jackets and, two of them, soft broad-brimmed hats. These clothes are virtually indistinguishable from those of merchant seamen and even naval ratings of the same period

SOME FOREIGN VISITORS

Among the Victorian and Edwardian sailing ships in British ports there were, of course, many foreign visitors, some of which were so characteristic in their rigging and construction of their places of origin as to be unmistakeable to seamen who might do no more than catch a glimpse of the upper parts of their masts. The great American schooners, the distinctive French schooners with their roller-reefing top-sails, the French luggers which survived unchanged from the eighteenth into the twentieth century, Dutch vessels and German vessels, Italian brigantines, Greek polaccas, were all to be seen in British ports. Among the most common visitors were the Scandinavian schooners, particularly those from Denmark, which by the Edwardian period had developed their ultimate hull form, with round full bows and flat transom sterns.

88 *opposite* The four-masted schooner, *Joseph B. Thomas*, built at Thomaston, Maine, U.S.A., in 1900 and seen being towed down the Avon at Bristol, was typical of the great four- and five-masted schooners built in New England, which represented the ultimate development of the merchant sailing ship in the nineteenth century. They were frequent visitors to British ports

89 *above* By way of contrast, the French schooner *La Mouette*, of Tréguier, with her great single square topsail equipped with an efficient roller reefing mechanism, was characteristic of the numerous schooners from Brittany which visited the ports of the south-west and the Bristol Channel

90 *above* These fine three-masted luggers were also characteristic of Brittany and were occasionally seen in British ports, such as Newlyn in west Cornwall. They look like smuggling luggers of the eighteenth century and were indeed very little different

91 *below* These two Norwegian wooden barques were photographed in 1905 lying in the Highbridge river in Somerset, which is now almost completely silted up. They were discharging timber cargoes. Scores of these Norwegian wooden square-rigged ships brought timber cargoes to Britain. These two are the *Triumph*, built in 1870, and the *Viking*, built in 1866

92 This remarkable photograph shows a Danish three-masted schooner with a big deck cargo of timber hove to in a full gale at sea. It is the only photograph I have ever seen depicting a small sailing vessel under these conditions. Notice that the schooner is riding perfectly happily; providing nothing goes wrong with her sails and rigging or her deck cargo, she is safe

93 Another Scandinavian vessel is this barquentine, almost certainly from Denmark, though she could just come from the southern part of Sweden. What marks her off from the rest of the world's shipping is the shape of her hull with the flat transom, like an ordinary boat, and the full bows with the convex stem. She was photographed running up the English Channel past the white cliffs. Notice the crew member standing on the foot ropes right out on the jib boom

94 This three-masted schooner is also Scandinavian, but almost certainly Swedish. She is anchored and drying her sails off Appledore in North Devon before starting to discharge her timber cargo into sailing barges. It is possible to date the photograph before 1896

THE ROYAL NAVY

At the beginning of the Victorian era the Royal Navy still comprised predominantly wooden sailing vessels, little different from those which fought at Trafalgar. By the end of Edward VII's reign wood had given place to steel, sail to steam and there had been enormous technical changes in every direction. The photographs which follow show a few naval sailing vessels which survived in one way or another into the age of the camera.

95 *below left* This view was taken from the old semaphore tower at Portsmouth harbour and shows the bows of the *Seraphis,* one of the Indian troopships, in the foreground, with the *Duke of Wellington,* a steam auxiliary three-decker built at Pembroke Dockyard and launched in 1852, behind. A local trading ketch is sailing between the two naval vessels

96 *below right* This remarkable early photograph of a naval officer shows the garment mentioned in the 1832 regulations for officers' wear 'in undress at sea, a round jacket without skirts, and with the appropriate buttons'. The cap in his right hand was introduced in the same regulation. He is probably a lieutenant Royal Navy and he is seen on the quarter-deck of a sailing man-of-war in the early 1840s

97 Sir Charles Napier's fleet leaving Spithead for the Baltic in the early days of the Crimean War. Queen Victoria is passing through the lines in the Royal Yacht *Fairy,* clearly visible in the exact centre of the picture with steam coming from her two funnels

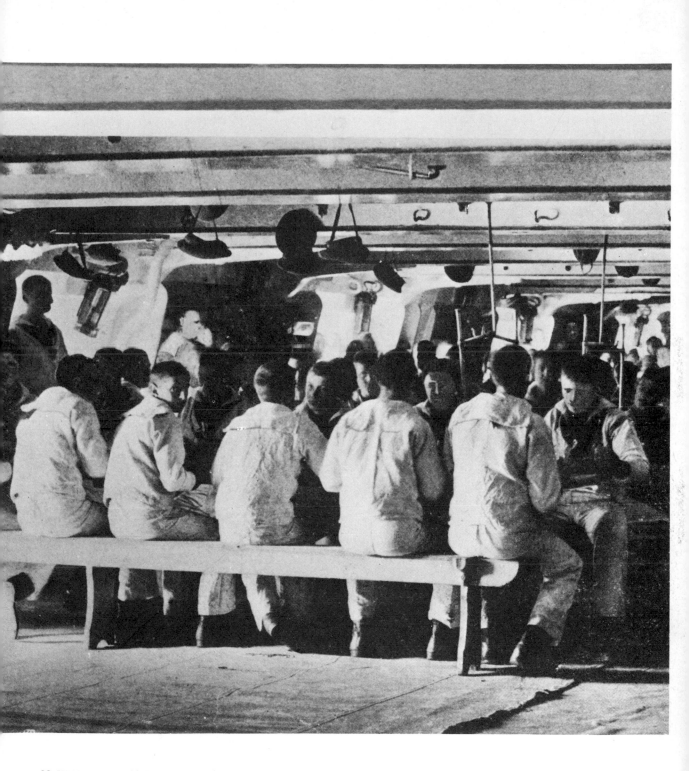

98 HMS *Impregnable* was a seamen's training ship anchored in the Tamar off Devonport. This view of one of her decks at dinner time gives a good idea of conditions in a sailing man-of-war in the middle years of Queen Victoria's reign

99 Portishead pier in North Somerset (now Avon) about 1885. It shows another boys' training ship, the *Formidable*, an old eighty-four-gun ship built at Chatham in 1825, which lay off the pier from 1869 to 1906. The pretty brigantine *Polly*, (see Plate 140) was her sea-going sailing tender. It also shows a Great Western Railway paddle steamer, the *Gael*, steaming through the anchorage, a topsail schooner, probably waiting for the tide to go up to Lydney or Gloucester, and two of C.J. King's tugs

100 The Royal Yacht *Royal George,* launched in 1817, being broken up at Portsmouth in 1905 after many years of service in retirement as a hulk

SAILING FOR A LIVING

Life at sea for most of the period covered by this book was by modern standards dangerous, arduous, uncomfortable and very badly paid. Greater economic prosperity, legislation, the requirements of insurance classification organisations and a developing social conscience all worked together towards the general improvement in conditions, just as they did to improve industrial conditions ashore. Generally speaking, at the beginning of Queen Victoria's reign a substantial number of the crews of vessels tended to come from the neighbourhood of the ports in which they were owned, and with small ships this continued right down to the end of the Edwardian era. But the crews of larger vessels tended to be recruited much more widely as increasing opportunity ashore and the development of steam vessels with generally better conditions of service provided alternative employment.

The professional sailing ship seaman was cut off from his fellow men and women and society ashore, sometimes beyond the point at which he could re-enter it. There is a brilliant picture of the crew of a sailing ship of the later part of the Victorian era in Joseph Conrad's *The Nigger of the Narcissus*

101 *opposite* The iron four-masted barque *Fort Jackson*, built in 1822, running before a strong wind and a heavy sea. The photograph was taken from the maintop and shows the master dressed in oilskins standing by the break of the poop. The crossjack, the lowest squaresail on the mizzen mast, has been furled and firmly secured in the gaskets

102 This is the finest photograph taken on board a big sailing ship in really heavy weather that we have ever seen. It illustrates more vividly than any other the, by modern standards, appalling industrial conditions in merchant sailing ships in Victorian and Edwardian times. The vessel is running under lower topsails and four of the crew are making fast the mainsail. The vessel is the *Inversnaid*, built in 1892 and later renamed *Garthsnaid*

103 *above* The full-rigged ship *Macquarie* is braced up on the starboard tack in a smooth sea with a breeze blowing, a passenger is strolling on the main deck and a seaman is cleaning out one of the boats. These are ideal sailing conditions

104 *opposite* This is the view the man at the wheel got when he looked aloft on board the schooner *Jane Banks,* (see Plate 143) running dead under her two square topsails and flying squaresail, foresail, mainsail and mizzen, but without her gaff topsails

105 *left* Two young mates of merchant ships in a posed photograph taken in a studio in the late nineteenth century to illustrate navigation with a sextant

106 *below* Sailmaker at work on board the iron full-rigged ship *Loch Tay*, built in Glasgow in 1869

107 *right* A successful merchant shipmaster of the 1850s. He is believed to have been master of a vessel in the North American timber and emigrant trade from the west of England

108 *right* 'Daddy' Johns, the ferryman, setting the mizzen on the Instow ferry boat about to cross to Appledore in the early years of this century, while an earnest young passenger takes the helm

109 A group of men and boys on Appledore quay in north Devon in early Edwardian times. They are all seamen, bargemen or boatmen. The man standing with a telescope and bowler hat is Joseph Cann. Notice the stooping woman on the slipway. Her presence does not seem to be causing any particular interest

110 Fishermen of Staithes in Yorkshire

THE SHIPBUILDERS

These photographs show different aspects of the building and repairing of wooden sailing vessels. This was a great industry in Victorian times and wooden ships were built almost anywhere where there was tidal water. Very little capital was needed to start a shipyard beyond the basic stocks of timber. Large wooden vessels were built with hand tools and no machinery. Iron and steam ship-building required much greater initial investment. The large sailing vessels were built at the centres of the new industry, particularly on the Clyde and the north-east coast

111 *left* Alexander Hall and Company were famous builders of clipper ships. This photograph shows two of their smaller vessels in frame, that is with their skeletons nearly complete but not yet planked up. The *Coulnakyle* on the left went into the China trade, the vessel on the right is the *Natal Star*. The names of all the men are known, from William Hall, Snr, standing hatless with legs apart and left hand in waistcoat pocket, to John Cruickshank, the office boy at the left hand of the two seated figures on the right hand side of the photograph. In the year in which this photograph was taken, 1862, these men built six wooden merchant sailing ships

112 *above* Laying the keel for a fishing vessel at St Ives in Cornwall in the early years of this century, with what appears to be the benefit of a good deal of advice from friends on the beach

113 *left* The schooner *Two Sisters* being planked up at the yard of T. Smart & Co. of Bosham, Sussex, at the beginning of the 1880s. Bosham was then a locally important port with a shipbuilding and repairing industry; now it is a fashionable yachting centre. The *Two Sisters* is being built on hard ground alongside a marine railway or patent slip, used for hauling out vessels for repair

114 *left* Here the *Two Sisters* is shown fully planked-up, but her masts have not yet been stepped and it will still be some time before she is ready to launch. Because of her peculiar position by the side of the repair slip she will have to be launched on the crest of a very high spring tide

115 *opposite top* This is the completed schooner *Two Sisters* as she was for most of her working life. As you can see, she was a long narrow vessel and she is lying in Dover harbour with her mainsail and foresail set. Her upper and lower square topsails, her staysail, standing jib, boom jib and flying jib are all loosed and ready to set. She survived in trade until the 1930s and was not broken up until after the Second World War

116 *opposite bottom* These are the men who worked at the shipyard of James Goss of Calstock in Cornwall. The ships were actually built on the other side of the river in the parish of Bere Ferrers in Devon. James Goss, the master shipwright, is sitting with arms folded in the middle of the group with his sons Harry and Lewis on either side of him, his grandson James Lowther to the left seated in front and Tom Goss seated to the right. Goss's yard built smacks and barges for trade on the Devon and Cornish coasts and a ketch called the *Garlandstone*, which was launched in 1909 and is still afloat preserved at Porthmadog in North Wales.

117 *above* Despite a good deal of research neither the name of this brigantine nor the date on which she was launched at Appledore in North Devon have been determined. But the launch was clearly an important one; the whole yard gang is assembled with many friends and relatives. The photograph was taken just short of the moment of launching. The lady concerned holds the bottle in her hand and the tape with which it is secured to the vessel is clearly visible. Stocks of timber lie around in the yard and school children are clustered at a safe distance near to the camera

118 *opposite top* This is the three-masted schooner *Mary Lloyd* about to be launched from the yard of D. & G. Williams at Rotten Tare, Porthmadog in north Wales in 1894. The *Mary Lloyd* is one of the magnificent schooners built at Porthmadog in the twenty-two years between 1891 and 1913 for the salt fish trade from Newfoundland to the Mediterranean and to Britain. Here the person who is performing the launch, who appears to be a young girl, is actually in the act of swinging the bottle against the side of the stem. The *Mary Lloyd* was sunk by a German raider off the coast of Brazil in 1917

119 *opposite bottom* The successful completion of a vessel was often celebrated with a party for those who had worked on her, given by the shareholders, particularly if they included some of the more prosperous elements in the local society. This party was given at Appledore but again the name of the vessel is not known. She was probably one of a series of three-masted schooners built on the Bell Inn slip at Appledore in the late 1890s and the first years of Edward VII's reign

120 *above* When a vessel was finished, almost at once the endless work of maintaining her began. Most shipbuilding yards made more money out of repairs than they ever did out of new building. But with the smaller ships a lot of work was done by the crews themselves. This view of Appledore Quay at about the turn of the century shows a man at work shaping a pine spar into a topmast for a ketch. In the background is a three-masted barque waiting to enter the Richmond dry dock, which is just out of sight around the corner, for repairs

121 Some of the crew of the schooner *Tankerton Tower* of Faversham, built at Whitstable in 1884, tarring the seams, that is, filling in the cracks between the planking with coal tar to prevent the oakum caulking, or sealing, from coming out

122 *above* In this photograph the crew of a Brixham trawler with some further assistance are doing rather more. They are driving in fresh caulking with the special tools used for this process, as well as tarring. DH 121 *Dauntless*, the vessel nearest the camera, was built by Samuel Dewdney at Brixham in 1885. DH 407 *Roebuck* in the background was built by J.W. & A. Upham in 1896, also at Brixham. The photograph was taken between that year and 1902 when the prefix DH was replaced by BM for Brixham vessels

123 *below* This schooner, the *Nikita*, owned at the time by John Westcott of Plymouth, was holed in collision with a steamer off Ilfracombe in September 1894. She is here shown with local boats around her in the early stages of salvage. She was raised and repaired and eventually wrecked at Holyhead in 1917

CANADIAN-BUILT

Despite the great number of merchant sailing ships built in Britain in Victorian and Edwardian times the British shipping industry was very dependent on Canadian shipyards. Since shipbuilding tended to be a slow process, it was most valuable in times of prosperity to have ready-made ships available for purchase off the shelf, and the Canadian shipbuilding industry went some way to fulfill this need. Labour tended to be cheap in Canada as also was timber, and free sites for shipbuilding were easy to find. The ships were very well built and Canadian builders could see themselves through periods of depression by employing their ships in the timber trade to Britain, which was protected by duties placed on Baltic timber.

124 *below* Very many sailing ships were built in Prince Edward Island, which in relation to its small size and population was the most productive shipbuilding area in Canada and at times was probably building more ships for Britain than any other place outside Britain. This photograph shows the fine three-masted barque *Gulnare*, built in Prince Edward Island in 1873, and later owned in Norway. She is lying in Cumberland Basin, Bristol, deep laden with a timber cargo

125 *opposite* In this photograph a shore boat is just coming up to the brigantine *Raymond*, built in Prince Edward Island in 1874. The *Raymond* was the last of these Canadian-built ships to remain afloat in British waters. She survived until the Second World War

126 Typical of the schooners built in Prince Edward Island for sale to British owners is the *Troubadour*, built near the island's capital, Charlottetown, in 1867 and photographed in the Bristol Channel off Portishead about the year 1900

127 The *Troubadour* was an ordinary Victorian topsail schooner, like the vessels lying on the left- and right-hand sides of this picture. In the centre is something entirely different. She is the *Swordfish*, built in 1885 by John Ramsay at Summerside, Prince Edward Island for James William Richards of New Bideford, and photographed at the end of her maiden voyage. This fine, powerful schooner with her big hull and simple rigging represents an interesting trend in the later development of the sailing ship in world trade which was pioneered in Prince Edward Island. She is quite different from the ordinary British schooners with which she lies. Vessels like the *Swordfish* were very successful and sailed all over the world. She herself was stranded on Buccoo Reef, Trinidad, in August 1892 and totally lost

WRECKS AND DISASTERS

Sailing ships ended their careers in many diffrent ways. Some were broken up, though the expense of breaking up a small wooden ship was often greater than the profit that could be made by selling the scrap which came from her, so many small vessels were simply laid up in quiet creeks and backwaters and allowed to fall to pieces there. Some ships were lost by fire at sea, some by storm at sea, sinking in the open ocean. A much larger number than should have been were lost without trace, simply missing. They sailed from one port towards another and were never heard of again in those days when there was no radio and no air searches. Ships sailing to Australia or from Australia back to Europe could easily be completely out of touch for three or more months on end.

A large number of sailing ships were wrecked. They went aground or on the rocks and were so badly damaged that they either broke up where they lay, or if salved never went to sea again.

128 Wrecks in Scarborough Bay: from left to right, the brig *Lily*, the brigantine *Black-Eyed Susan* of Bideford, built at Maryport in 1853, and the schooner *Bosphorous*

129 *above* We do not know the name of this wooden merchant ship lying on the repair grid of Cumberland Basin, at Hotwells, Bristol, in 1880, but from the chain plates for the rigging she was clearly a three-masted barque and from the shape of her hull and the arrangement of her deckhouses Canadian-built, quite probably in Prince Edward Island. She has the appearance of having been dismasted at sea, but certainly of being by no means beyond repair

130 *opposite* The barque *Firth of Cromarty*, formerly a full-rigged ship, but the yards have been stripped from her mizzen mast and replaced with a gaff and boom sail. She is ashore on the Scots coast in 1898. She carried a cargo of whisky and was bound from Glasgow towards Australia. It is said that some of the whisky was still being drunk locally twenty years later

131 The Brixham trawler *Harry* firmly stuck on the rocks near Porthcurno in Cornwall in 1910. Her crew was saved, but the *Harry* herself was totally lost. She was built at Brixham in 1904. Notice the photographer with a heavy hand camera standing on the rocks in the foreground

132 The Severn trow *Arabella* of Gloucester, lost in the entrance to Ilfracombe harbour with her crew of four and two local men in the autumn of 1895. She was washed up high and dry on the southern side of the entrance to the harbour and here at low tide she is being visited by curious local people. The Severn trow was the sailing barge of the River Severn and the Bristol Channel. *Arabella* was built far inland at Saul on the Berkeley canal in 1864

TECHNICALITIES

In this book we have had to use technical terms because it is quite impossible to write, even in the simplest way, about Victorian and Edwardian sailing ships without doing so. The technology of sailing ships was extremely complicated and there are a large number of books on the subject. Some people who have enjoyed the photographs in this book may want to know and have illustrated the proper definitions of the technical terms we have used to describe sailing ship rigs, such terms as barque, barquentine, brig and so on. In this section these rigs are illustrated and defined in simple terms.

During the nineteenth century it became the general practice to describe sailing ships by the disposition of their masts and sails rather than by their occupations or the shapes of their hulls, as had in general been the practice before. The rigs became standardised, more or less. In this section we use the terminology in general use among merchant seamen at the end of Queen Victoria's reign.

We have to use the terms 'square-rigged' and 'fore-and-aft rigged'. A square-rigged mast was one divided by its supporting rigging into three distinct parts, a short lower mast, a topmast, and a topgallant mast. From each of these masts sails were set from yards which could be trimmed on the fore side of the mast only, so that the wind always acted on the same surface of the sails, the after surface. The fore-and-aft rigged mast was in two parts, a long lower mast and the short topmast. A gaff and boom sail which could be trimmed only abaft the mast was set from the lower mast and a gaff topsail or sometimes one or more square-sails was set from the topmast. The gaff sail received the wind on either side according to its direction, relative to the direction in which the vessel was sailing.

A square-rigged vessel had at least one square-rigged mast, as defined above. A fore-and-aft rigged vessel had her masts all fore-and-aft rigged as defined above. In the later nineteenth century certificates were granted under the Merchant Shipping Acts which qualified masters to take charge of fore-and-aft rigged vessels only or steamers only or to take charge of all types of vessel, including square-rigged ships.

These technicalities come to life in the photographs and descriptions which follow.

133 *opposite* Joseph Conrad was the mate of this full-rigged ship, *Torrens*, when this photograph was taken from one of her boats in the course of a ninety-day passage to Australia in the 1890s. The full-rigged ship was the queen of sailing vessels, square-rigged on all her three, or occasionally four, masts and her origins can be traced back to the middle 1400s. The *Torrens* has divided topsails, upper and lower, set from her topmasts, that is the second and third sails up each mast. In the 1870s divided topsails replaced the huge single topsails set from the topmasts which were difficult to handle unless the vessel had a very large crew

134 This full-rigged ship is a naval vessel and therefore has a very large crew. Naval vessels, for this reason and to maintain tradition, kept the deep single topsails until sails were abandoned altogether. The *Volage* was an iron corvette, cased with wood and equipped with steam engines as well as sails, built in 1869 at Blackwall by the Thames Shipbuilding Company. In 1894, with her consort the *Active,* she was the last naval ship to leave Portsmouth unaided by steam. She was not sold out of the Navy until 1904. In this photograph, besides almost all her normal working canvas she sets studding sails, extra sails set outside the ordinary squaresails, rarely used by merchant ships after the 1870s and never probably worth the cost and the effort of setting them

135 In the late nineteenth century, as the scale of industry and the size of cargoes increased, the standard rig for the big sailing vessel, now grown too large for the three-masted ship rig, became the four-masted barque, square-rigged on three masts, the fore, the main and mizzen, fore-and-aft rigged on the last, called the jigger. The four-masted steel barque was an efficient ship by the standards of her times, even in competition in some trades with contemporary steamers.

This four-masted barque is the *Bidston Hill*, built in 1886, owned in Liverpool and lost off Cape Horn in 1905.

136 *above* The three-masted barque with fore and main mast square-rigged and mizzen with a gaff and boom sail developed in the eighteenth century. For the greater part of Queen Victoria's reign this was the most popular rig for medium-sized merchant vessels and by the 1880s barques were of anything from 200 to 2,000 tons and were to be met with in almost every trade all over the world. This barque is the *Asta,* built in Nova Scotia, photographed outward bound in the Bristol Channel off Portishead. She has a Cardiff pilot on board and is towing his cutter

137 *opposite top* The barquentine was square-rigged on her foremast and fore-and-aft rigged on her two or more other masts. This was the last classic sailing ship rig, developed both in Europe and in the United States in the early Victorian period from an early nineteenth century British experiment. This barquentine is the *Waterwitch,* built at Poole in 1871 and the last square-rigged merchant sailing ship to earn her living carrying cargoes from a home port in Britain. This photograph again illustrates an important point. Not all sailing vessels were always smart and well kept up. The old *Waterwitch* here is wearing a second-hand suit of squaresails on her foremast which do not fit her and what looks like a spare topmast staysail in serving as the flying jib

138 *opposite bottom* By way of contrast this photograph shows the *Waterwitch* at anchor with her sails furled. The upper topsail yard is lowered down on the lower topsail yard, its normal position when the sail is not set. The *Waterwitch* made her last voyage with cargo under the British flag in 1936

139 *left* The brig shared with the full-rigged ship the distinction of the longest lineage among sailing vessels. She had two masts and was square-rigged on both. Brigs were very common indeed until the 1870s, when they passed out of use because they needed big crews in an era of increasing manpower costs. We have deliberately chosen this rather run-down old brig with her deep single topsails, photographed in the Indian Ocean many years ago. In the real workaday world of Victorian times perhaps the majority of vessels were like this one

140 *left* The brigantine in Victorian England was a two-masted vessel, square-rigged on the foremast and fore-and-aft rigged on the main. Brigantines were usually the smallest type of square-rigged sailing vessel and a well-designed brigantine with her masts and sails nicely proportioned could be among the most beautiful of sailing ships. This vessel is the *Polly*, built at Brixham in 1864 and used as a training ship for boys

141 *above* In Britain the term schooner was used for a two- or three-masted fore-and-aft rigged vessel with squaresails set from yards on the fore topmast. In the early years of the Victorian era the schooner rapidly became the most popular rig for small sailing vessels in this country. This handsome vessel is the *Snowflake*, built at Runcorn in Lancashire in 1880. She is shown in this photograph almost becalmed off the Cornish coast. Notice the seaman on his way out along the bowsprit to make fast the flying jib. This has just been taken in because the vessel will shortly be entering port

142 *left* This photograph also shows the *Snowflake*, but under very different circumstances in a strong breeze at sea. Her main topsail and flying jib have been taken in and her mainsail reefed

143 *below* Three-masted schooners were built in the eighteenth century, but the rig did not become common in Britain until the 1870s, after which it was enormously popular until the end of sailing shipbuilding just before the First World War. This three-masted schooner is the *Jane Banks*, a famous vessel built at Porthmadog in 1878

144 *below* By way of contrast this photograph shows spectators idly watching the three-masted schooner *Result* lying in the river at Bridgwater some years before the First World War. She was built in Ulster in 1893 and survived seventy years of sailing to be preserved by the Ulster Folk Museum

145 *overleaf* In the United States and Canada conditions in the long-range coastal trades made it possible to develop huge schooners with four, five and six masts which were in some ways the most efficient merchant sailing vessels ever built. They were frequently seen in British ports. This vessel is the *Mary H. Diebold* shown coming up to an anchor

146 The ketch had a tall mainmast and a smaller mizzen, both rigged with gaff and boom sails. In the later Victorian era ketches became extremely popular both as cargo-carrying vessels and for fishing. They were economical to build and to sail and easier to work than a schooner. This handsome ketch is the *H.F. Bolt*, built at Bideford in 1876

147 Right through the Victorian and Edwardian periods single-masted sailing vessels, usually referred to as smacks, were commonly met with in the short range coastal trades. This vessel is the *Volunteer*, built at Padstow in 1860, sailing out of Porth Gaverne in North Cornwall deep laden with slate she has loaded from carts on the open beach. She has a little breeze astern and is setting her gaff topsail. The men in the rowing boats, who have contracted to tow her out, have not got much work to do. The photograph was taken in the 1870s

148 *above* The peculiarly-shaped dipping lug sail which had to be partly lowered and then reset on the other side of the mast each time the vessel went about was the most common type of sail used in small and medium-sized fishing vessels in the Victorian period. This vessel is the *Alaska*, owned in Sennen Cove in west Cornwall, sailing hard in a strong breeze in Mounts Bay

149 *opposite* For centuries the spritsail was the commonest sail used in working boats. It is extremely cheap and simple and many boatmen could cut it out and rig it up themselves. This photograph shows 'Daddy' Johns of Instow, North Devon (see Plate 108) sailing his handsome sprit-rigged boat across from Appledore

150 During the Victorian period the spritsail was gradually replaced in many areas by the working lug, which, unlike the dipping lug in Plate 148, did not have to be dipped when the boat went round. This photograph shows a working lugsail of the type which replaced the spritsail of Appledore in the 1890s. Our own family boat, built in Cornwall, was rigged at Appledore in this fashion and long experience with her has shown that despite its apparent inefficiency the sail is thoroughly practical for a small traditional working boat